# Digging Deep

Paul Mason

**Digging Deep**

Text: Paul Mason
Publishers: Tania Mazzeo and Eliza Webb
Series consultant: Amanda Sutera
Hands on Heads Consulting
Editor: Kirstie Innes-Will
Project editor: Annabel Smith
Designer: Leigh Ashforth
Project designer: Danielle Maccarone
Permissions researchers: Lumina Datamatics
Production controller: Renee Tome

**Acknowledgements**
We would like to thank the following for permission to reproduce copyright material:

Front cover: Nathan Christepher Palmer/peopleimages.com/Adobe Stock Photos; p. 4: Arterra Picture Library/Alamy Stock Photo; p. 5: Evgeny/Adobe Stock Photos; p. 6 (top): Peter Hermes Furian/Adobe Stock Photos, (bottom) FatCamera/E+/Getty Images; p. 7: KATERYNA KON/SCIENCE PHOTO LIBRARY/Getty Images; Index page, Content page, p. 8 (top): Andramin/Shutterstock.com, (bottom left): Hadynyah/E+/Getty Images, (bottom right) (Title page): Johan Holmdahl/Shutterstock.com; p. 9 (top): GraphicsRF.com/Shutterstock.com, (bottom): SShuddho/Shutterstock.com; pp. 10, 11: Vadim Sadovski/Shutterstock.com; p. 12: Thomas Faull/iStock/Getty Images; p. 13 (top): AlexLMX/Shutterstock.com, (bottom): Vince Streano/Corbis Documentary/Getty Images; p. 14 (top): Wasilij Martynow/Shutterstock.com, (bottom): Photoillustrator/Shutterstock.com; p. 15 (top): severjn/Shutterstock.com, (bottom): Shchipkova Elena/Shutterstock.com; p. 16: Newscom/Alamy Stock Photo; p. 17 (top): Fly_and_Dive/Shutterstock.com, (bottom): Robert Gilhooly/Alamy Stock Photo; p. 18: Alena Veasey/Shutterstock.com; p. 19 (top): Alex Potemkin/iStock/Getty Images, (bottom): Pavliha/iStock/Getty Images; p. 20: Dorling Kindersley/Dorling Kindersley RF/Getty Images; p. 21 (top): Wlad74/Shutterstock.com, (middle): IR Stone/Shutterstock.com, (bottom left): vvoe/Shutterstock.com, (bottom right): PitukTV/Shutterstock.com; p. 22 (top left): Macrowildlife/Shutterstock.com, (top right): Kitthanes/Shutterstock.com, (bottom): Bloomberg/Bloomberg/Getty Images; Backcover page, p. 23: (top) New Africa/Adobe Stock Photos, (bottom): Bjoern Wylezich/Shutterstock.com; p. 24 (top): xpixel/Shutterstock.com, (bottom): engel.ac/Adobe Stock Photos; p. 25 (first row): Hans Wismeijer/Shutterstock.com, (second row): Heroya77/Shutterstock.com, (third row): N-sky/Shutterstock.com, (fourth row): NetPix/Shutterstock.com; p. 26 (top): David Fleetham/Alamy Stock Photo, (middle): Todor Stoyanov/Shutterstock.com, (bottom): Nguyen Quang Ngoc Tonkin/Shutterstock.com; p. 27 mauritius images GmbH/Alamy Stock Photo; p. 28: VW Pics/Universal Images Group/Getty Images; p. 29 (top): Andy Myatt/Alamy Stock Photo, (middle): Matt Crossick/Alamy Stock Photo, (bottom): Imago/Alamy Stock Photo; p. 30: HUGO INFANTE/AFP/Getty Images.



**NovaStar**



ISBN 978 0 17 033500 3

**Cengage Learning Australia**
Level 5, 80 Dorcas Street
Southbank VIC 3006 Australia
Phone: 1300 790 853
Email: aust.nelsonprimary@cengage.com

For learning solutions, visit **cengage.com.au**

Printed in China by 1010 Printing International Ltd
1 2 3 4 5 6 7 29 28 27 26 25

*Nelson acknowledges the Traditional Owners and Custodians of the lands of all First Nations Peoples. We pay respect to Elders past and present, and extend that respect to all First Nations Peoples today.*

# Contents

# Journey to the Centre of the Earth

*Journey to the Centre of the Earth* is a famous adventure story written by Jules Verne, a French novelist. It is narrated by the character of Axel, a young student who joins his uncle, a professor of geology, on a daring expedition deep below ground to learn about Earth.

In the passage of text below, a nervous Axel stands on the edge of a volcano crater in Iceland, and stares down a deep, dark hole. He's about to go on a quest to the very centre of Earth.

> **"I leaned over a rock ... and looked down. My hair stood on end, my teeth chattered, my limbs trembled ... while my head was in a sort of whirl ..."**
>
> *Journey to the Centre of the Earth*, 1864

Axel finds the Central Sea in his journey to the centre of the Earth.

At the time Jules Verne wrote the book, some people believed that Earth was hollow. In Verne's story, the underground world has a mushroom forest, a giant sea and fighting dinosaurs!

Like Verne, people have long been fascinated with what lies underneath our feet. It isn't possible to journey to the centre of Earth. But if it were, just how far down would we have to go? And what would we discover?

Time to start digging ...

A geologist studies a rock sample.

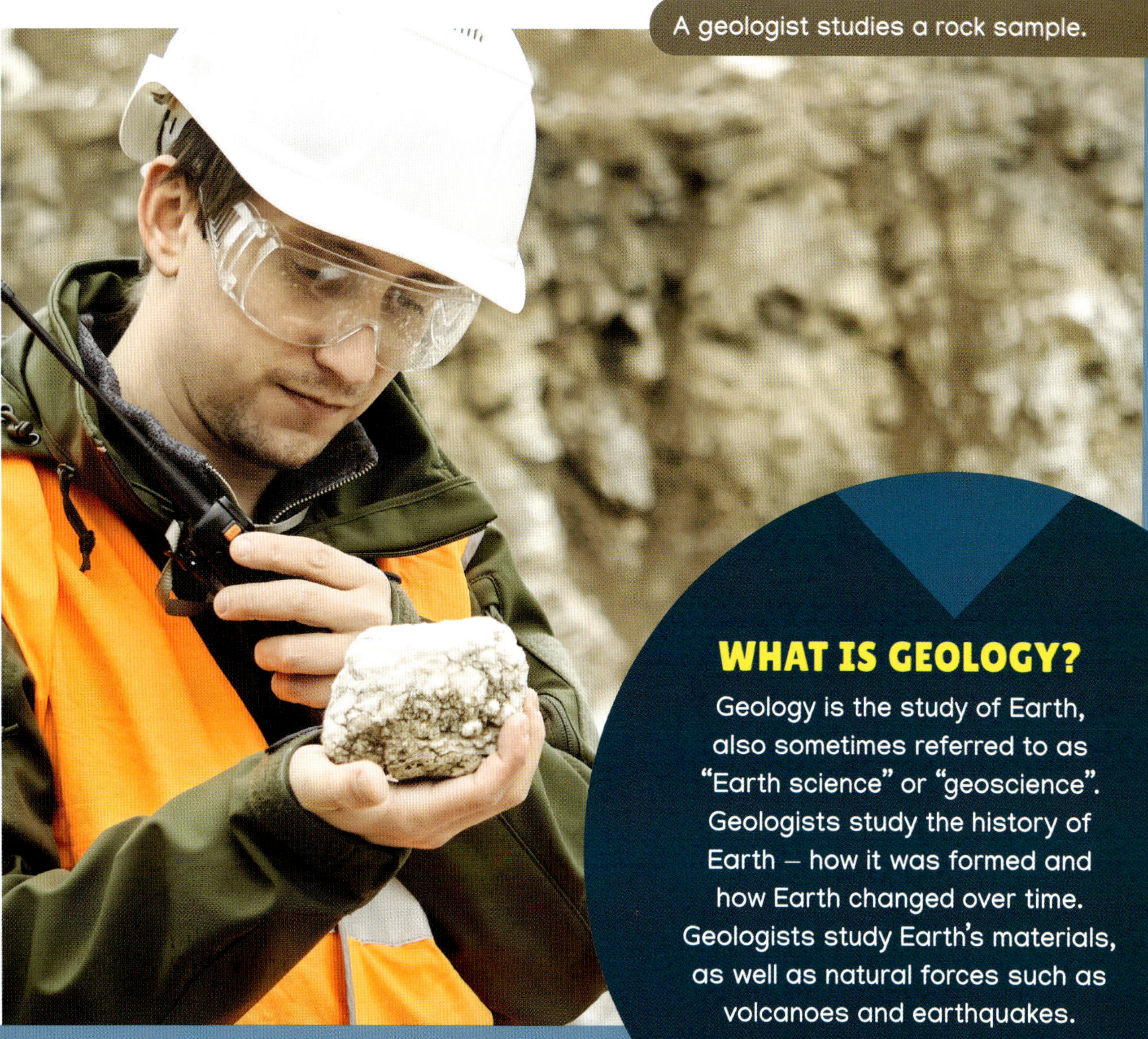

## WHAT IS GEOLOGY?

Geology is the study of Earth, also sometimes referred to as "Earth science" or "geoscience". Geologists study the history of Earth – how it was formed and how Earth changed over time. Geologists study Earth's materials, as well as natural forces such as volcanoes and earthquakes.

# Earth's Layers

To understand what Earth is made up of, imagine a giant boiled egg. Like the egg, Earth has layers.

Earth has four main layers. The ground that we stand on is the outer layer of Earth, known as the **crust**. Think of it like the shell of the egg. Beneath that there is the **mantle**, the egg white. At the centre are Earth's outer and inner **core** – the egg yolk.

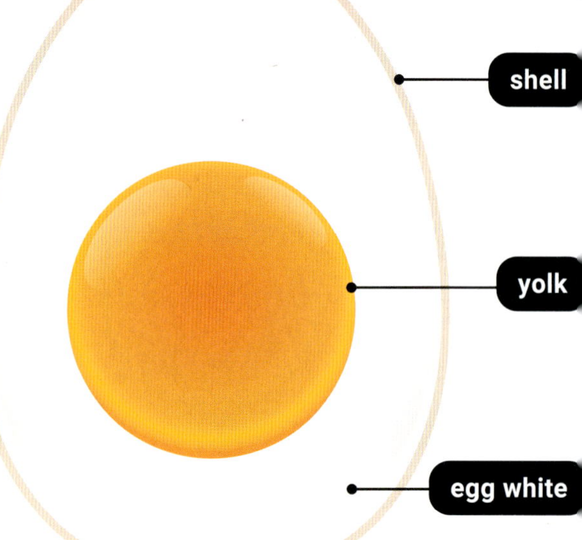


The ground we walk on is known as the crust.

If it were possible to cut out a piece of Earth, it might look like this.

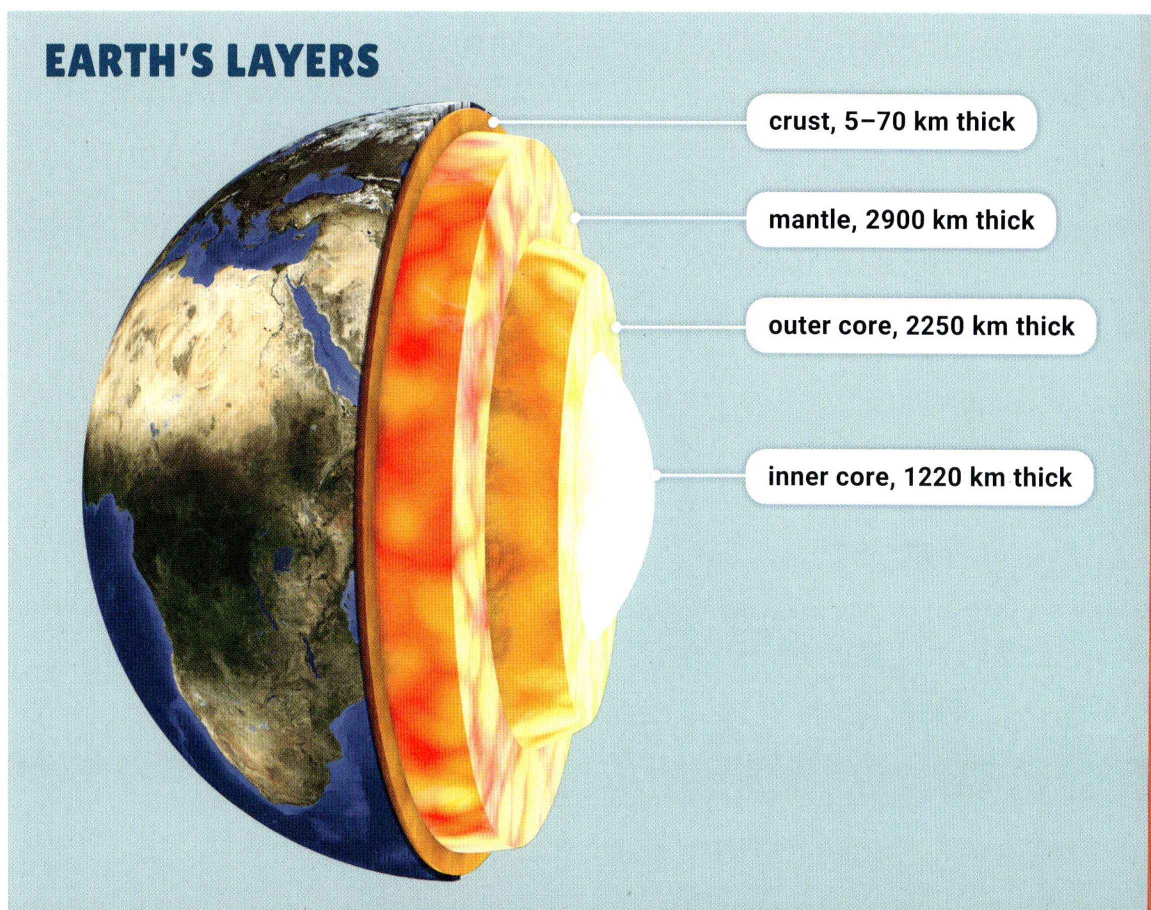


Earth's layers are different in size. The centre of Earth is roughly 6400 kilometres down. The deeper the layer, the hotter it is.

Earth's layers are made up of different materials. For example, the crust is solid, but the outer core is liquid. The crust and mantle are made of rocks and **minerals**, while the inner and outer cores are made of metals.

Although the layers are different, each layer of Earth is interconnected. Changes deep below the ground can have impacts on life on the surface.

# Crust

The hard outer layer of Earth is called the crust. It is made up of rock and minerals, and is the thinnest of all the layers. In fact, the crust makes up only 1 per cent of Earth's **mass**. But the crust is also home to all of life on Earth.

Earth's crust is made up of two types: the continental crust and the oceanic crust. The **continental crust** is what people think of as land. The thickness of the crust changes. In some parts, like the high mountain ranges of the Himalayas in Asia, the crust is at its thickest, over 70 kilometres thick.

The part of the crust covered by the sea is called the **oceanic crust**. The oceanic crust is thinner, between 5 and 10 kilometres deep.

## THE OCEANIC AND CONTINENTAL CRUSTS

The oceanic crust is much thinner than the continental crust.

The continental crust is thick in places like the Himalaya mountains (left). The oceanic crust below the sea (right) is thinner.

# Plate Tectonics

The crust isn't just one piece. It is split into several large slabs, or pieces, called **tectonic plates**. These plates fit together a bit like a puzzle. The plates move very slowly, over a long period of time.

## EARTH'S TECTONIC PLATES

The tectonic plates lie beneath the continents and oceans of the world and move in the directions shown.

"Plate tectonics" is the theory that explains the movement of the tectonic plates that causes them to collide and push against each other. This force creates mountains and trenches, and also causes earthquakes and volcanic activity.

A volcano forms when two tectonic plates collide and the heavier plate slides beneath the lighter plate.

# Mantle

Below the crust layer is the mantle. The mantle is the biggest portion of the planet. It is thought that the mantle makes up about 84 per cent of Earth's mass.

The mantle is made of rock and minerals. The top part of the mantle is mostly solid, and along with the crust makes up Earth's outer layer. Together, the top part of the mantle and the crust are known as the lithosphere.

Below the lithosphere, the mantle is hot – around 1300 degrees Celsius. This temperature causes the rock to partly melt – a bit like softened candle wax. This **molten** layer of the mantle is called the asthenosphere.

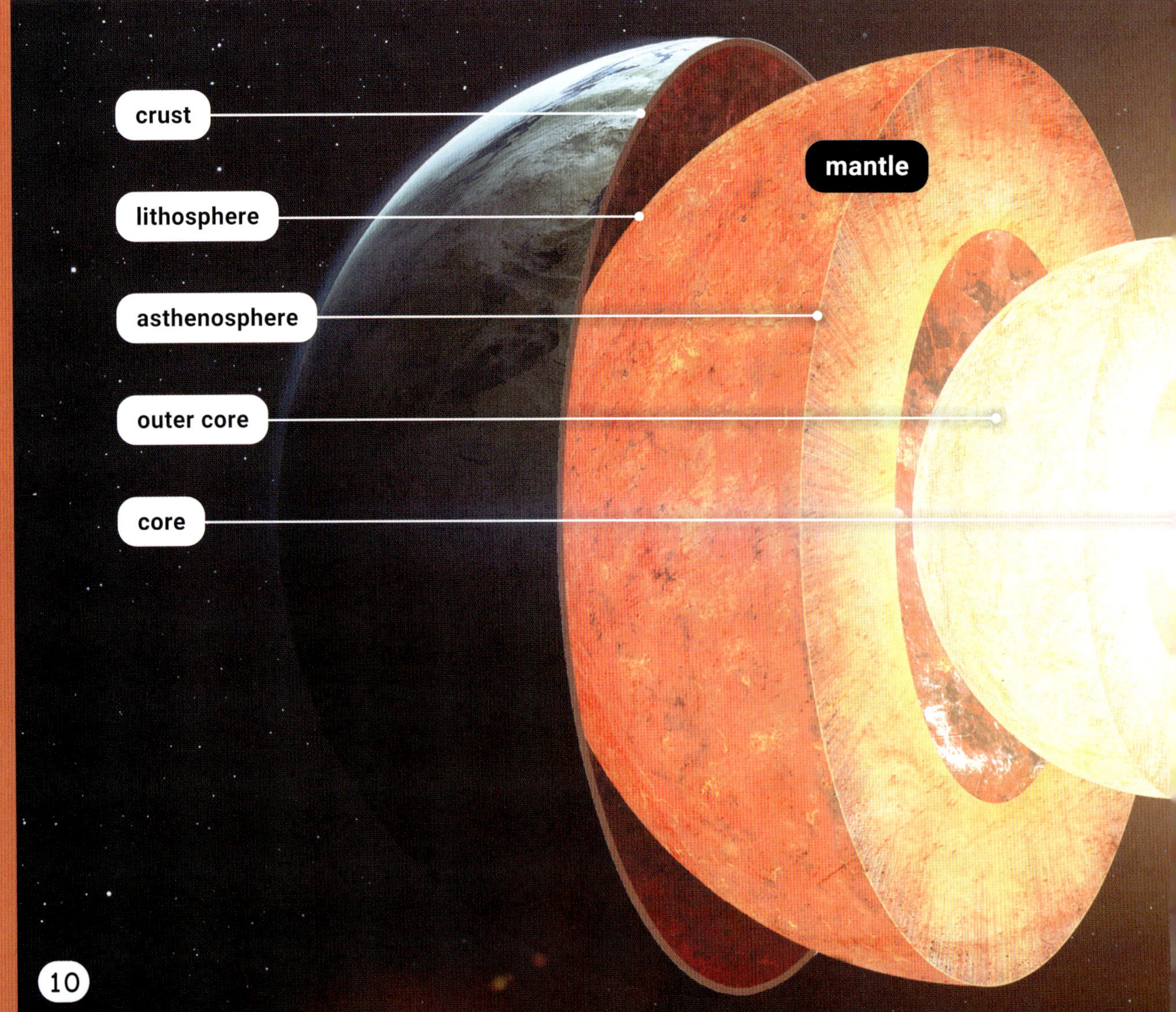

Earth's tectonic plates "float" on top of this soft, changeable layer. Scientists believe this is what allows the tectonic plates to move. Think back to the boiled egg – if the boiled egg was cracked, the broken pieces of shell could move around on top of the soft egg white underneath.

## THE THICKEST LAYER

The mantle is around 2900 kilometres deep. That's about 327 Mount Everests stacked on top of each other.

The mantle makes up the bulk of Earth.

# Core

At the centre of Earth is the core. The core is made up of metals, mostly iron and nickel.

The outer core is liquid due to the extreme heat – around 4500 degrees Celsius. But hotter still is the inner core. Here, it gets to around 5200 degrees Celsius. In fact, it is thought that Earth's inner core is almost as hot as the surface of the Sun!

But unlike the outer core, the inner core is solid. This is because the inner core is under huge pressure. It has the weight of all the other layers pressing down on it.

Of course, it is impossible for scientists or researchers to get that far down. So how do they know about the core and Earth's layers?

The inner core of Earth is almost as hot as the surface of the Sun.

# Discovering More About Earth

## Studying Waves

One way that scientists learn about Earth's layers is by studying earthquakes. When earthquakes take place, **seismic waves** travel through the Earth. The waves behave differently depending on what kind of materials they move through. For example, waves travel faster when they pass through dense materials such as granite rock. By studying the waves, scientists can learn what makes up the different layers.

Scientists use an instrument called a seismograph to measure the seismic waves. They can find out where the earthquake took place, as well as learn more about the materials that make up Earth's layers.

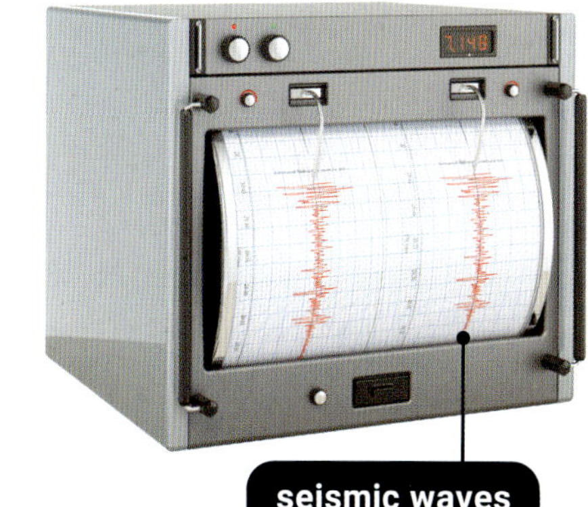


Different kinds of rocks and minerals reflect seismic waves in different ways.

# Drilling Deep

To find out more about the planet and Earth's geological history, scientists also drill down into the ground. Researchers hope to one day reach the mantle. So, just how deep have people drilled?

## The Deepest Hole in the World

In 1970, a project called the Kola Superdeep **Borehole** began in Russia. The plan was for scientists to go further beneath Earth's surface than ever before. It was not easy drilling such a deep hole, even if the hole was only about 20 centimetres wide. The team had to drill very straight. The temperature within Earth got hotter the deeper they went.

For around 20 years, the team in Russia drilled down and down. Eventually Earth became so hot, parts of the drill and pipes started to bend out of shape and the project had to stop.

The only sign of the Kola Superdeep Borehole today is the remains of its metal cover.

### THE KOLA PENINSULA

The Kola Superdeep Borehole is in the remote Kola Peninsula in Russia – within the Arctic Circle.

During the Kola Superdeep Borehole project, scientists were able to pull up rock samples that helped them learn about the materials in the crust. They even discovered fossils of ancient **plankton** buried deep down in the rock.

The Kola Superdeep Borehole still holds the record for the deepest hole in the world to be drilled. It goes down about 12.2 kilometres deep, but it isn't even close to the mantle. Today, all that is left of the borehole is a metal cover.

The Kola Superdeep Borehole is depicted on a Russian stamp.

The buildings around the Kola Superdeep Borehole lie abandoned.

# Deep Sea Drilling

Japan is a country that experiences lots of earthquakes. To try to predict future quakes and protect lives, it is important for scientists to learn more about what causes them. *Chikyu* is a Japanese deep sea drilling ship designed to do just that.

*Chikyu* carries special drilling machinery and 10 kilometres of drill pipe to allow it to bring back samples from deep in the ocean floor. *Chikyu* has special underwater thrusters, or propellers, that keep the ship steady while it drills. There are laboratories on board for scientists from around the world to study the samples.

In 2014, *Chikyu* drilled a borehole over 3 km deep into the ocean floor.

In 2011, a strong earthquake hit Japan, causing a destructive tsunami. The centre of the earthquake was in the ocean near a **fault** where two tectonic plates meet.

The Tohoku earthquake in 2011 caused huge waves that devastated coastal areas.

The *Chikyu* team drilled into the earthquake zone to take measurements and collect samples. They learnt that one of the factors that made the earthquake so powerful was that the clay inside the fault was extremely "slippery", causing increased movement.

*Chikyu* aims to one day reach as far down as the mantle. However, the *Chikyu* scientists will not have to drill as deep as the Kola Superdeep Borehole. (Remember, the oceanic crust is much thinner than the crust found under land.) The *Chikyu* aims to drill through around 7 kilometres of ocean floor to get to the mantle.

Up to 200 people can work aboard the *Chikyu*.

# Mining for Resources

Research isn't the only reason to dig deep. Important materials lie below Earth's surface. People use those materials to build things we use every day.

How do people get to school or to work each day? If they catch the bus or travel by car, these vehicles are made from metals such as steel or aluminium. The glass in the windscreens and windows comes from sand. If they walk, the pavement is probably concrete — which is made from things like sand and stone.

All these materials and more come from Earth. Mining is the process of getting natural, raw materials from Earth's crust.

### ANCIENT MINES

People have been mining for thousands of years. It is thought that the oldest mine in the world was dug in Africa more than 40 000 years ago. People dug the mine to get a special red clay to use for rock paintings.

We use metals extracted from the earth every day in our modern lives.

When the materials are close to the surface of the crust, mining companies might dig an open-pit mine. The ground is either drilled or blasted with explosives. To get at the materials, mining companies then dig a series of “benches” or layers, creating a giant, open hole.

If the material is deep inside the crust, mining companies dig an underground mine with **shafts**, ramps, levels and rooms below the surface.

Underground mines can be dangerous places to work in.

## THE LARGEST OPEN PIT

The largest open-pit mine in the world is in Utah, USA. The mine is a massive 1.2 kilometres deep and 4 kilometres wide. It could fit 38 soccer pitches end to end across the top!

Kennecott Bingham Canyon Copper Mine

Underground mines are more difficult and expensive to dig than open-pit mines. There are dangers working deep underground. Explosives are used to blast the rock. Weight presses down on the tunnels. It is hot, dark, and there can be poisonous gases.

## PARTS OF A MINE

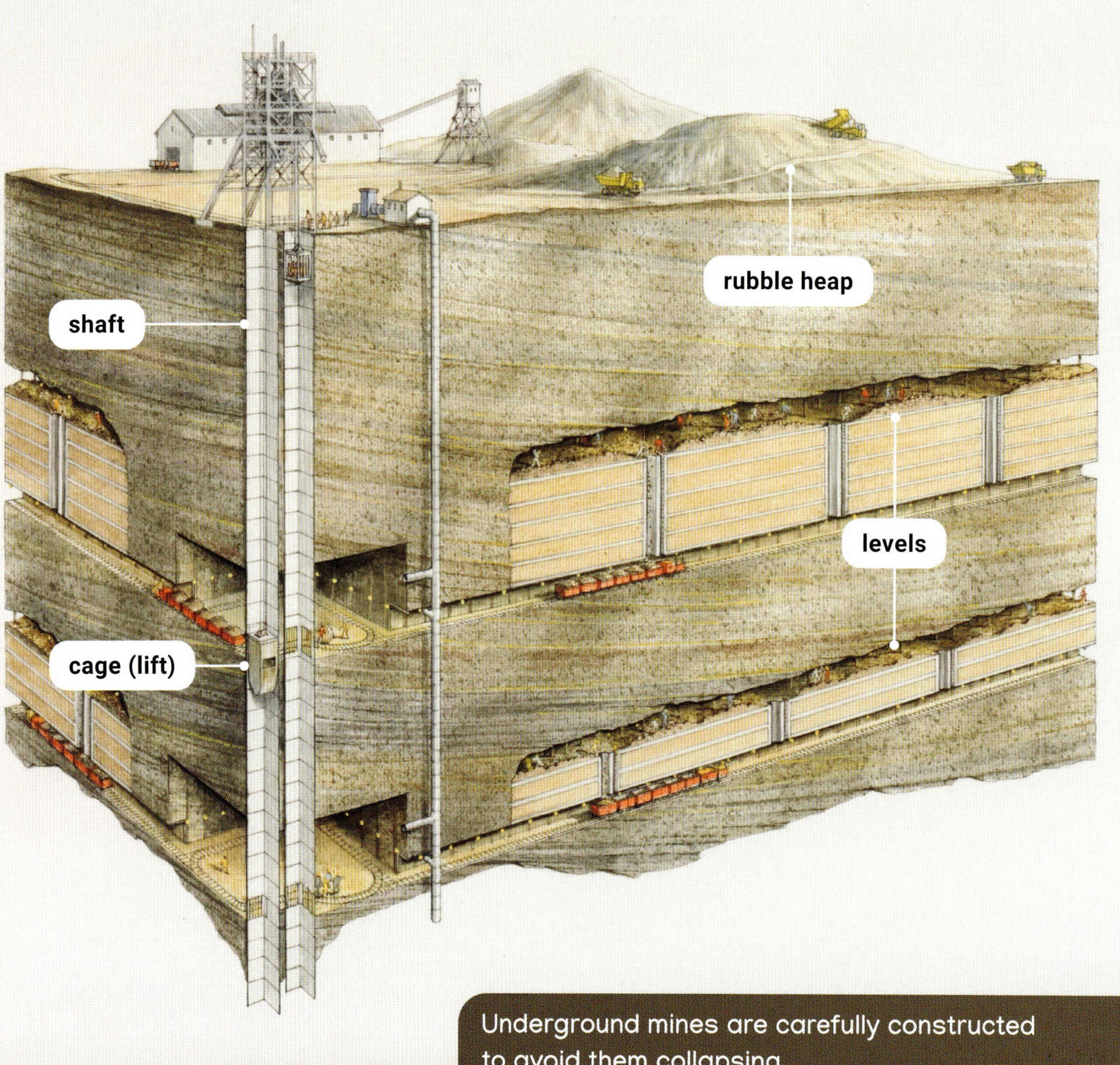


Underground mines are carefully constructed to avoid them collapsing.

# What Do People Mine?

Lots of useful materials are mined from Earth.

## Iron

iron

Iron makes up 5 per cent of Earth's crust and most of the core. Iron is the most used metal in the world. It gets turned into steel and is used to build all kinds of things, from skyscrapers to refrigerators to cruise ships.

Iron is used to build skyscrapers in cities.

## Copper

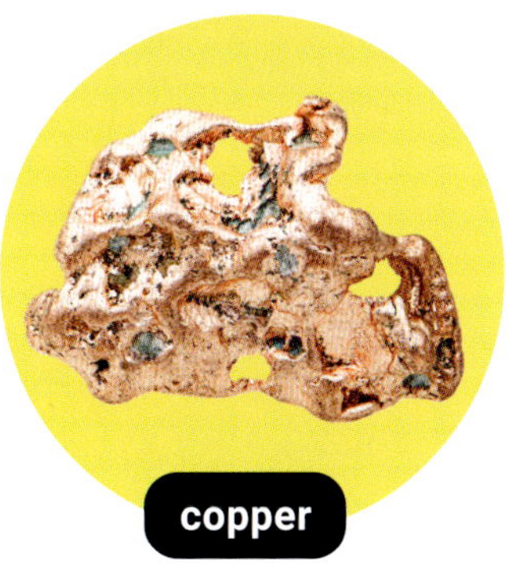

copper

copper wire

Streaming a favourite show? Using a console to game? That's possible thanks to the metal called copper. Copper is soft, but strong. It is easy to shape and doesn't rust. Copper is a good **conductor** of electricity. Copper is in all kinds of electrical devices, and copper wire is used to connect them. Copper is also used to make household water pipes.

Remember that giant, open-pit mine from earlier in the book? It's a copper mine.

# Gold

Gold is a valuable metal. With its special colour and shine, gold is highly prized. Gold has a long history of use in jewellery, as well as being made into coins for trade. (The first gold coins were made over 2500 years ago in an area that is now Turkey.) Like copper, gold is also used in computers and electronics as a conductor.

a gold nugget

gold bars

## THE WORLD'S DEEPEST MINE

The world's deepest mine is the Mponeng gold mine in South Africa. To get at the gold, the tunnels reach about 4 kilometres below the earth. That is so far down that it's deeper than twelve Eiffel Towers stacked on top of each other. To get from the bottom to the surface takes the miners over an hour and a half!

This miner is working 3 kilometres beneath the surface.

# Gemstones

Gemstones are precious minerals. Gemstones are rare, and that makes them highly valuable. Gemstones come in colours such as blue, like a sapphire, or bright red, like a ruby. The most well-known gem is probably the diamond. Diamonds form in the heat of the mantle.

Jewellers cut the raw gemstones into particular shapes for jewellery.

Another gem that forms deep in the mantle is peridot. This gemstone has a rich green colour. Peridot is brought to Earth's surface by volcanoes. So, holding a diamond or a peridot is like holding a piece of the mantle!

peridot

# Coal

The most mined material in the world is coal. Coal is a **fossil fuel**. Some coal can be mined from Earth's surface, but much of the world's coal comes from underground. The countries with the largest reserves of the world's coal are the USA, Russia and Australia.

coal

Burning fossil fuels is the leading cause of climate change.

Coal is burned to make electricity and is currently the largest source of fuel for making power. But burning fossil fuels like coal releases harmful gases into the atmosphere. This leads to a rise in Earth's temperature and causes **climate change**.

# Mining and the Environment

Producing fossil fuels isn't the only impact mining can have on the environment.

| Mining Activities (Causes) | What is the Impact? (Effects) | |
|---|---|---|
| Giant holes are excavated from Earth. Sometimes whole mountains are removed. | This changes the landscape and can harm natural habitats. |  |
| Not all material dug out of mines is useful. | Mining can create large amounts of rock and other waste, some of it toxic. |  |
| Mining produces dust, and mining machinery creates fumes. | Pollution is released into the air. |  |
| Mining can use harmful chemicals such as cyanide. Metals are released from the ground. | Chemical waste and metals can leak into water sources. |  |

There are laws around mining – such as rules about what mining companies have to do with chemical waste so waterways stay safe. The aim is to try to reduce the environmental damage and remove resources in a way that is responsible.

To try to limit the burning of fossil fuels, many countries are switching to natural, **renewable energy**. Wind turbines convert wind energy into electricity, and **solar panels** use the energy of the Sun.

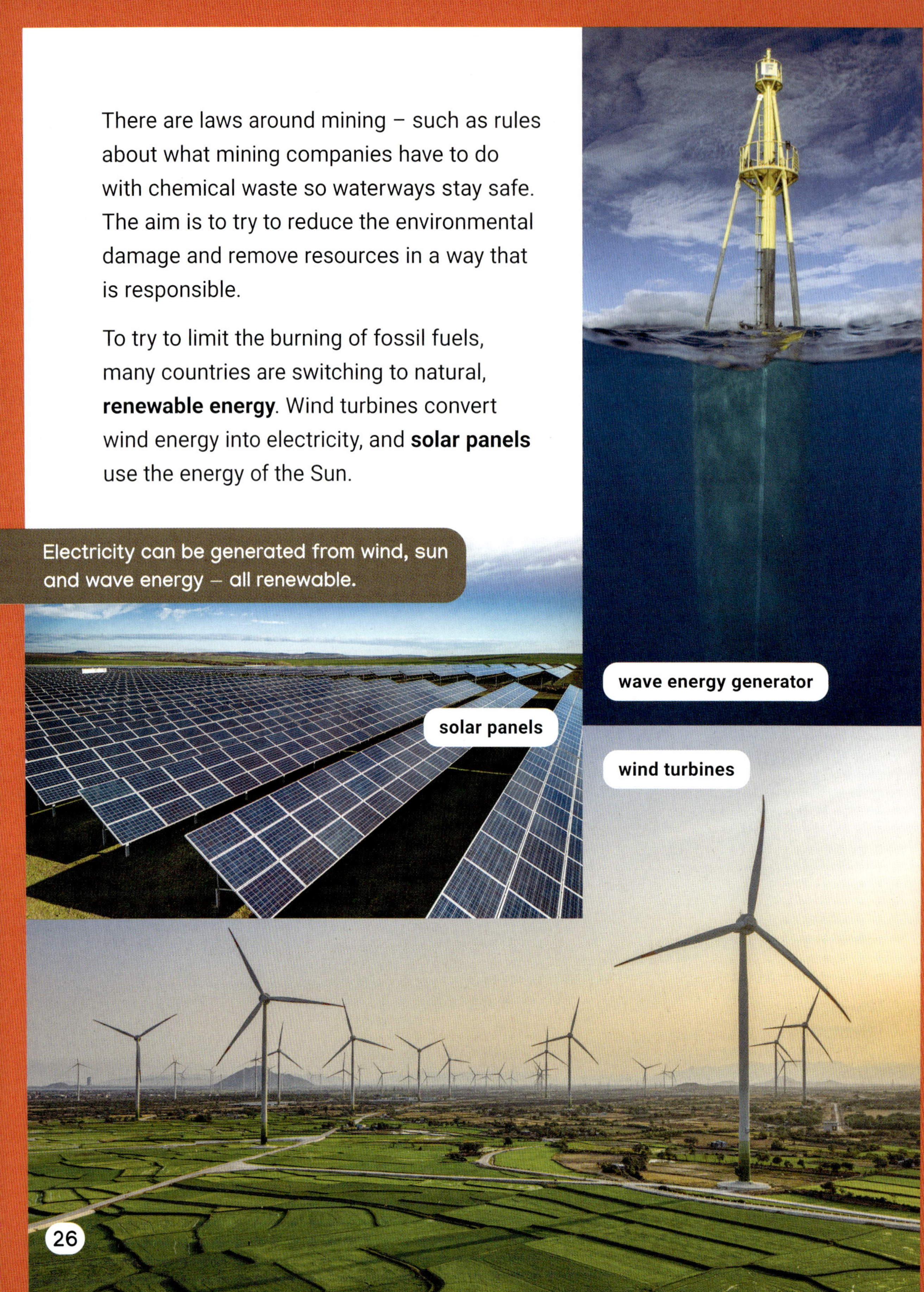


Electricity can be generated from wind, sun and wave energy – all renewable.

# Continuing to Dig

There is much still to discover about Earth. Of course, unlike Axel in Jules Verne's famous book, we can't journey to the centre of the planet to find out. (We do know it isn't hollow and there are no fighting dinosaurs!)

But through scientific exploration, we can continue to learn more about the layers of Earth and the forces beneath the surface, such as the movement of tectonic plates. Studying our planet teaches us how Earth has changed in the past, and can perhaps help us to better understand the impacts of climate change we face now. It is important for us to keep learning.

Scientists continue to study Earth and its layers.

# The Rescue of the "33"

In the afternoon of 5 August 2010, at a gold and copper mine called the San Jose Mine in Chile, a group of miners working underground noticed vibrations in the mine. Some also noticed small rock falls.

There was a big bang. When the dust cleared, the men saw that part of the mine had collapsed. The main way out of the mine was blocked, trapping them 700 metres below ground!

The miners were trapped deep underground.

To survive deep underground, the 33 trapped men knew they needed to work together as a team. Fearing they would be stuck underground for a long time, they shared what little food and water they had, only having a meal every second day.

Up on the surface, rescue workers began drilling small boreholes and sending down **probes**, hoping to find signs of life below ground. Relatives of the miners set up a camp called *Campo Esperanza* – "Camp Hope".

A huge camp was set up at the mine to support the rescue.

After 17 days without any contact, the rescuers found a note tied to one of the probes they pulled up. It said: "We are well in the shelter, the 33."

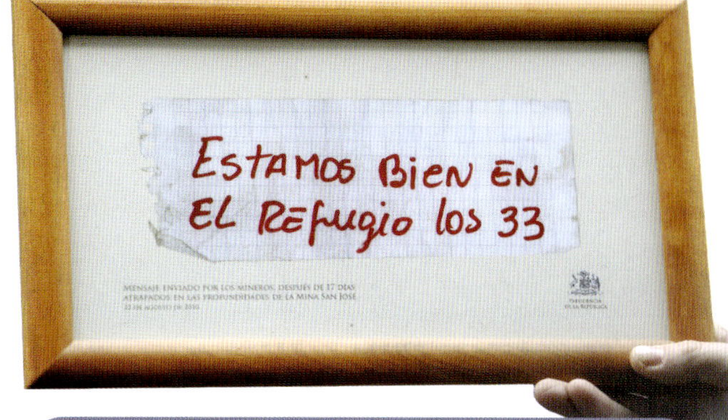


Rescuers were surprised to discover that 33 people were still alive in the mine.

Soon, the rescuers were able to send food and water down the boreholes. The miners could communicate with their families, too.

The rescue workers started drilling bigger holes to get the men out. They made special metal capsules, or containers, ready to bring them up.

Metal capsules were used to rescue the miners.

Down below, the trapped miners worked hard, too, taking it in turns to clear rock and make the walls of the mine stronger.

At last, one of the rescue tunnels reached the men. One by one, the miners were strapped into a capsule. The capsule was slowly raised to the surface, a journey that took around 15 minutes for each miner.

The amazing rescue was watched around the world.

Finally, on 13 October 2010, after 69 days trapped deep in the mine, the last of the "33" was finally free.

The amazing rescue was cheered by everyone at Campo Esperanza, and by millions watching around the world.

# Glossary

| | |
|---|---|
| **borehole** (*noun*) | a deep, narrow hole bored, or drilled, in the ground to help locate and remove materials |
| **climate change** (*noun*) | changes in weather patterns from a rise in Earth's temperature as a result of human activities such as burning fossil fuels |
| **conductor** (*noun*) | a material that allows heat or electricity to flow through it |
| **continental crust** (*noun*) | the part of Earth's crust that makes up the continents or land |
| **core** (*noun*) | the very dense centre of the Earth |
| **crust** (*noun*) | the outermost layer of Earth |
| **fault** (*noun*) | a fracture or break in Earth's crust |
| **fossil fuel** (*noun*) | a fuel – such as coal, oil and natural gas – that comes from the ancient remains of plants and animals buried underground |
| **mantle** (*noun*) | the mostly solid interior of Earth |
| **mass** (*noun*) | the amount of matter in something |
| **minerals** (*noun*) | materials that are inorganic – they do not come from plants or animals |
| **molten** (*adjective*) | heated to a high temperature so it melts |
| **oceanic crust** (*noun*) | the part of Earth's crust that is beneath the sea |
| **plankton** (*noun*) | tiny sea organisms |
| **probes** (*noun*) | tools used to explore or investigate |
| **renewable energy** (*noun*) | energy that comes from natural sources such as sun, wind and water |
| **seismic waves** (*noun*) | waves or vibrations that travel through the Earth |
| **shaft** (*noun*) | a vertical tunnel in a mine |
| **solar panels** (*noun*) | devices that use heat and light from the Sun to make electricity |
| **tectonic plates** (*noun*) | pieces of Earth's crust that are always moving |

# Index